OUR
SOLAR SYSTEM

Written by **Ian Graham**

TWO-CAN

First published in Great Britain in 1991 by
Two-Can Publishing Ltd
27 Cowper Street
London EC2A 4AP

Text copyright © Ian Graham, 1991
Editorial and Design by Lionheart Books, London
Editor: Denny Robson   Picture Research: Jennie Karrach
Media Conversion: Peter MacDonald, Una Macnamara and Vanessa Hersey
Studio Artwork: Radius

Printed and bound in Hong Kong

British Library Cataloguing in Publication Data

Graham, Ian
    Our Solar System
    1. Solar system
    I. Title
    523.218

ISBN 1-85434-093-X

Photograph Credits:
p.6-7 NASA. p.8 NASA/Starland Picture Library. p.9 NASA. p. 10 NASA. p.11 NASA. p.13 (top right) NASA/Starland Picture Library. p.13 (left) Ian Graham. p.14 NASA. p.14-15 Julian Baum. p.15 NASA. p.16 Julian Baum. p.17 NASA. p.18-19 Julian Baum. p.19 (top left) NASA. p.19 (top right) NASA. p.20 Julian Baum. p.21 US Naval Observatory. p.22 Ian Graham. p.30 NASA. p.31 NASA/Ian Graham. Cover photo NASA/Science Photo Library.

Illustration Credits:
All illustrations by Chris Forsey and Peter Bull except those on pages 24-28, which are by Graham Humphreys of Virgil Pomfret Artists.

CONTENTS

All words marked in **bold** can be found in the glossary

OUR SOLAR SYSTEM

Our Solar System is the Sun and everything that is affected by the Sun's **gravity**. The planets, the **moons** that circle the planets and a variety of other objects, including **comets**, move the way they do because of the Sun's gravitational attraction.

There are nine planets. Our planet, Earth, is the third out from the Sun. The planets are all quite different. Their differences are largely the result of their different distances from the Sun.

We call the planets that are closer to the Sun, including the Earth, the inner planets. They are small rocky worlds. The outer planets are much larger and are made from much lighter materials. All but two planets, Mercury and Venus, have moons in orbit around them.

▼ The Sun and the family of planets trapped by the Sun's powerful gravitational forces. The Sun is much bigger than the planets that orbit it. In fact, the Sun contains more than 99 per cent of all the mass, or material, in our Solar System.

1 Mercury   6 Sun
2 Venus   7 Saturn
3 Earth   8 Uranus
4 Mars   9 Neptune
5 Jupiter   10 Pluto

SYSTEM FACTS

● The orbits of the planets lie in a flat plane, except for Pluto's orbit, which is tilted compared to the others.

● All of the planets orbit the Sun in the same direction.

● Our Solar System is about 12,000 million km (7,500 million miles) across.

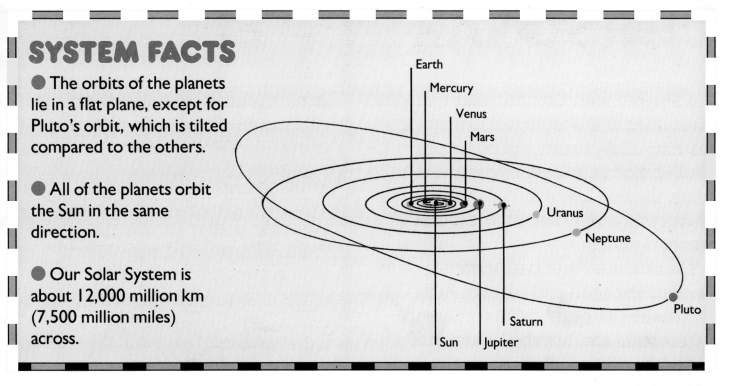

Earth
Mercury
Venus
Mars
Uranus
Neptune
Pluto
Saturn
Sun   Jupiter

THE SUN

The Sun is a star. Compared to many other stars in the night sky, it is quite ordinary. Other stars are bigger or smaller, hotter or colder than the Sun. To us, the Sun looks the biggest star of all, but this is only because it is the nearest to Earth.

The Sun is a huge ball of gases, mainly hydrogen and helium. At its centre the temperature and pressure are so great that hydrogen **atoms** are forced together to form helium atoms by a process called nuclear fusion. When they do this, they release a huge amount of **energy** in the form of heat and light. The Earth receives a tiny fraction of the Sun's total energy output, but it is enough to warm the Earth and to provide the light that green plants need to survive.

SUN FACTS

● The Sun is 1.4 million km (900,000 miles) across and the temperature at its centre is 15 million degrees centigrade.

● The Sun is divided into six layers. The surface of the Sun that is visible from Earth is called the photosphere. The chromosphere and the corona form an **atmosphere** above this.

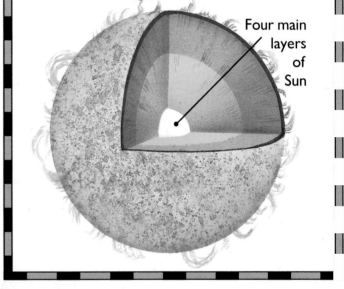

Four main layers of Sun

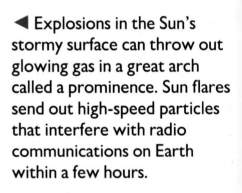

◀ Explosions in the Sun's stormy surface can throw out glowing gas in a great arch called a prominence. Sun flares send out high-speed particles that interfere with radio communications on Earth within a few hours.

▶ The corona, the outermost layer of the Sun's atmosphere, extends millions of kilometres into space. It is normally invisible, but when the Moon passes between the Earth and Sun, blotting out the Sun, the glowing corona is revealed.

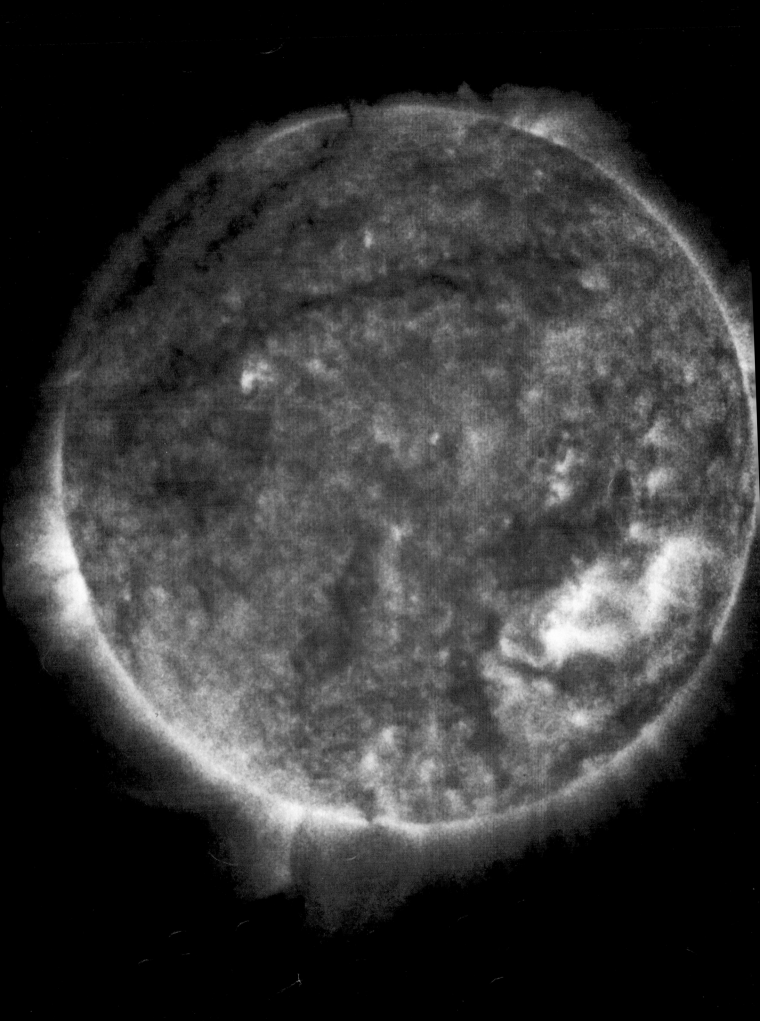

THE EARTH AND MOON

Our home planet, Earth, is as far as we know the only planet in our Solar System where life has evolved. It is also the only planet in our Solar System that has flowing water on its surface. Almost three-quarters of the Earth's surface is covered by water.

The pull of the Earth's gravity traps a layer of air called the atmosphere all around it. The Earth's rocky surface, or crust, is not as solid and stationary as it seems. It consists of a number of separate plates that move. Where they meet, they rub against each other. This is what causes **earthquakes** and **volcanoes**. The Earth's surface is also changed by the action of the wind, the rain and the tides.

▲ The Moon is much smaller and lighter than the Earth. Because of this, its force of gravity is weaker, about one-sixth of the Earth's. The Moon is unable to hold an atmosphere.

EARTH FACTS

● The Earth has a metallic core of nickel and iron. Its centre is solid, with a liquid outer core. A layer of rock called the mantle surrounds this, with a thin layer of lighter rocks on top, the Earth's crust.

● Above the Earth's crust is atmosphere, the layer of gases that lies between our planet and outer space – the cosmos.

● The Earth formed from material orbiting the Sun about 4.5 thousand million years ago.

MOON FACTS

● The Moon is the only world apart from the Earth that people have walked on. Twelve United States astronauts landed on the Moon between 1969 and 1972 in the Apollo missions.

● The Moon always shows the same face to the Earth because it spins around in the same time as it takes to orbit the Earth.

● The Moon's surface is covered by craters caused by rocks called meteorites crashing into it from space.

The tides – the twice-daily rise and fall in sea level – are caused by the Earth's satellite, the Moon. As the Moon orbits the Earth, its force of gravity pulls on the water under it and so raises the water level.

▲ Viewed from space, the Earth is the most colourful planet in our Solar System, with its blue oceans and brown land masses topped with white cloud. This photograph was taken from space by a weather satellite orbiting the Earth at a height of 36,000 km (22,500 miles).

Mercury is the closest planet to the Sun. The Sun is three times bigger in Mercury's sky than in Earth's sky. The side of Mercury that faces the Sun is heated to 500 degrees centigrade, hot enough to melt lead. As the planet turns away from the Sun, the night-time temperature plunges to minus 200 degrees centigrade.

MERCURY FACTS

● Mercury's day, the time it takes the planet to spin round once, is 59 Earth-days long. Its year, the time it takes the planet to go once round the Sun, is only 88 Earth-days long. So its year is only one-and-a-half Mercury days!

When the US space probe Mariner 10 flew past Mercury in 1974–5, it sent back pictures of a rocky planet, a third of the size of Earth and covered with craters that looked like our Moon's.

Venus is nearly the same size as the Earth, but it is a very different world. Its atmosphere contains mainly carbon dioxide and its surface is always hidden underneath clouds that are full of droplets of sulphuric acid. The pressure at its surface is nearly 100 times the pressure at the Earth's surface. Venus is too hot now to have water flowing over its surface. It may have had oceans once, but they must have evaporated a long time ago.

◄ This picture of Mercury is made up from several photographs taken by Mariner 10 as it approached the planet in March 1974. It shows Mercury's heavily cratered surface.

► This photograph of Venus taken by the US Pioneer – Venus Orbiter shows the planet's thick covering of cloud. The probe used **radar** to look through the cloud and see the surface.

VENUS FACTS

● The Soviet Union has landed space probes on Venus and taken pictures of its rocky surface. Its sky is orange-yellow.

● Venus is the brightest object in the night sky after the Moon.

MARS

Mars has fascinated people for thousands of years. Some ancient civilisations worshipped it as a god. Mars was the Roman god of war. In 1877 an Italian astronomer called Giovanni Schiaparelli drew a map of Mars. It caused a great stir because the planet was shown criss-crossed with what Schiaparelli described as channels.

At the beginning of this century, the US astronomer Percival Lowell also saw the channels, but he described them as man-made canals. For the next 70 years or so, scientists could not agree whether or not intelligent creatures lived on Mars. In the 1970s space probes visited Mars and finally discovered that there are no canals or intelligent creatures there at all.

▶ This photograph of Mars taken from Earth shows one of its polar icecaps, but little else can be seen. More detailed studies of Mars were made possible by space probes.

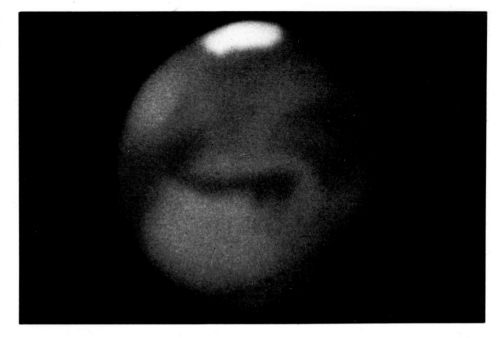

▼ This view of Mars, also called the Red Planet, shows Olympus Mons. This is a volcano 24 km (15 miles) high and 600 km (375 miles) across at the base, with a crater 80 km (50 miles) in diameter.

MARS FACTS

● Mars is half the diameter of the Earth and its force of gravity is weaker. Someone who weighs 50 kg (110 pounds) on Earth would weigh only 19 kg (42 pounds) on Mars.

● Mars has two moons, Phobos and Deimos.

● A Martian day is only a few minutes longer than an Earth-day, but the Martian year is 687 Earth-days.

● Mars looks like a red star in the sky. It is brightest every 780 days when it is on the other side of the Sun from the Earth. It then reflects most sunlight to Earth.

● The temperature on Mars during its summer ranges from −120°C at night to −43°C during the day. Mars is much colder than Earth because it is further from the Sun and its atmosphere is thinner.

◀ A US Viking Lander sits on the Martian surface. Two Viking spacecraft landed on Mars in 1976. Each spacecraft photographed the area around its landing site and tested the soil for signs of life, without success.

JUPITER

Jupiter is the giant of our Solar System's nine planets. More than 1,300 Earths would fit inside it. Jupiter is unlike any of the rocky inner planets, including Earth. It is a huge ball of liquid wrapped in gas clouds. It is mostly made of hydrogen and helium, just like a star. In fact, Jupiter seems to be a star that failed to 'turn on'. It was unable to attract enough material to create the high temperature and pressure at its core necessary for nuclear fusion to begin.

Jupiter's most obvious feature is its Great Red Spot. This is actually a storm that has been raging in Jupiter's atmosphere for at least as long as people have been observing the planet ... and that is over 300 years!

▼ Until the United States sent space probes to fly past the outer planets, Saturn was the only planet known to be encircled by rings. Then the Voyager spacecraft discovered rings around Jupiter (below), Uranus and Neptune.

JUPITER FACTS

● Jupiter is bigger and heavier than all the other planets added together.

● Jupiter has 16 moons. Two of them are larger than the planet Mercury.

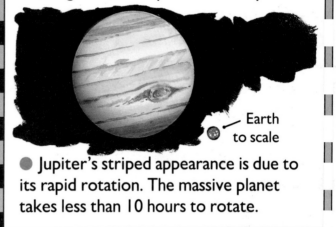

Earth to scale

● Jupiter's striped appearance is due to its rapid rotation. The massive planet takes less than 10 hours to rotate.

◀▼ The Great Red Spot is constantly changing. Three oval cloud systems formed in 1940. One is visible below the Great Red Spot in the photograph below. Left, an impression of a space probe plunging into the clouds.

SATURN

Saturn, with its flattened disc of rings, is the most spectacular planet in our Solar System. The rings change in appearance depending on whether they are tilted towards the Earth or have their edges facing the Earth. They seem to disappear when edge-on. Saturn is the second biggest planet in the Solar System. Like Jupiter, it is mostly liquid hydrogen. It has 18 moons. The largest, Titan, has a thick atmosphere of nitrogen gas.

▶ Saturn and its largest moons, compiled from Voyager photographs. The Voyager space probes discovered that the broad rings were actually hundreds of narrow ringlets.

SATURN FACTS

● Saturn is twice as far from the Sun as Jupiter and so it is a much colder world. It receives only one-hundredth as much heat from the Sun as the Earth does.

● Saturn is over 120,000 km (75,000 miles) across. That is almost ten times the diameter of the Earth.

Earth
to scale

▲ Some of Saturn's ringlets are held in place by the gravitational forces of nearby moons – nicknamed 'shepherd satellites'. The rope-like intertwining of some rings is also thought to be due to the shepherd satellites.

Each of the outer planets, Uranus, Neptune and Pluto, is strange for a different reason. Uranus lies on its side, with one pole and then the other facing the Sun. The poles are hotter than the **equator**, which must produce very odd weather conditions.

Neptune was thought to be similar to Uranus until Voyager 2 found it to be a much stormier planet.

Neptune's largest moon, Triton, has an atmosphere and a **magnetic field**, which are two features of a planet. It may be a planet captured by Neptune's gravity. Pluto's orbit is tilted to the orbits of the other planets and it also crosses inside Neptune's orbit.

▼ Voyager 2 one hour before its closest approach to Uranus. It passed within 107,000 km (66,000 miles) of the planet.

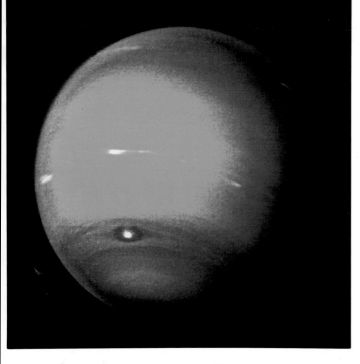

▲ An artist's impression of Pluto (bottom right), its moon Charon (top) and the distant Sun. By photographing Neptune through filters (left picture), Voyager measured the amount of methane gas in its atmosphere.

COLD FACTS

● Uranus and Neptune both consist of a ball of hydrogen and helium gases with a core of rock surrounded by ice. They are almost the same size, roughly 49,000 km (30,000 miles) in diameter.

● With a diameter of only 3,000 km (2,000 miles), Pluto is our Solar System's smallest planet. Some of the moons orbiting Jupiter, Saturn and Neptune are similar in size to Pluto.

● Little is known about Pluto, but it appears to be a frozen snowball of water and methane. It may have a rocky core.

COMETS, ASTEROIDS AND METEORITES

A broad band of rocky chunks called asteroids lies between the orbits of Mars and Jupiter. The asteroids range in size from grains of sand to rocks 1,000 km (600 miles) across. The largest are also called minor planets. They seem to be the ingredients of a planet that failed to come together.

▼ During the 1990s a spacecraft called *Galileo* will orbit Jupiter to study the planet. It is shown here passing an asteroid on its way.

DID YOU KNOW?

● Not all asteroids are found in the asteroid belt. The Apollo asteroids orbit close to the inner planets. Several of them have passed within a few million kilometres of the Earth. The Trojan asteroids are trapped at points on Jupiter's orbit where its gravity and the Sun's gravity balance each other.

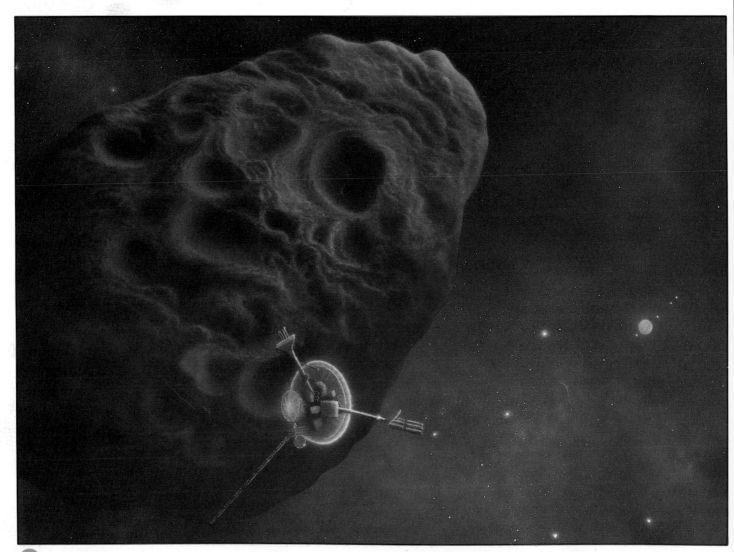

Comets and meteors are often seen from Earth. Comets are balls of dusty ice that orbit the Sun. The head of a comet is called the nucleus. Gas evaporating from this forms a cloud, the coma. Solar wind blows the tail away from the Sun. A meteor is a streak of light that is seen in the night sky for a moment and then disappears. Meteors are produced when a grain of dust enters the Earth's atmosphere and burns up.

▼ Comet Ikeya-Seki was visible with the unaided eye for several mornings in 1975. The coma and tail can be seen very clearly.

SPACE PROBE

Unmanned space probes, such as the Pioneer and Voyager spacecraft, have explored vast expanses of our Solar System. They have sent back spectacular photographs and valuable information by radio, from hundreds of millions of kilometres away in the outer reaches of the Solar System.

We know a great deal more about the Sun, the planets, their moons and even the origin of our Solar System thanks to deep space probes. The two Voyager space probes sent back over 30,000 photographs from Jupiter alone. They then went on to visit most of the outer planets.

▼ A space probe nears Saturn. Its dish aerial receives commands and sends information back to Earth. The long rods are aerials and an instrument boom.

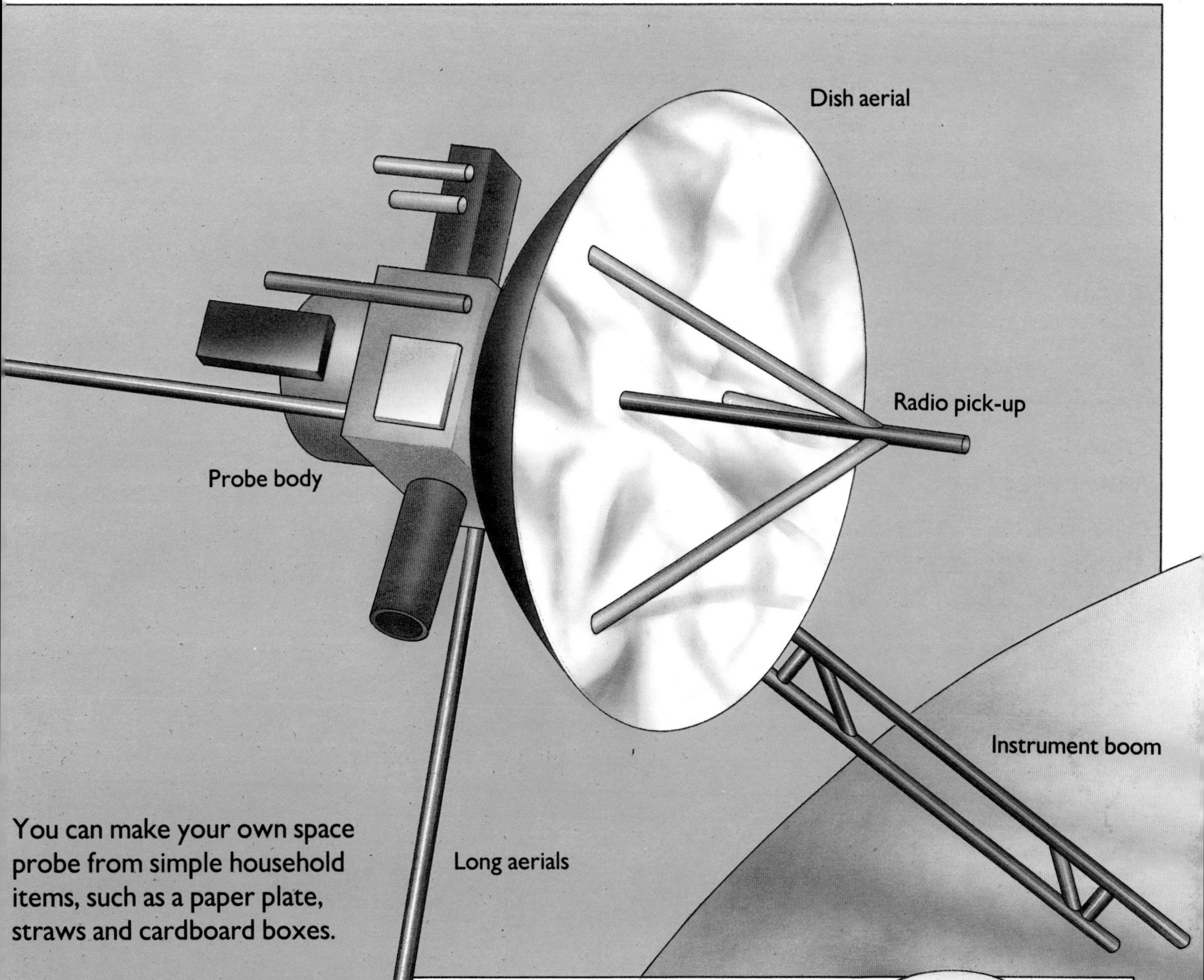

Dish aerial

Probe body

Radio pick-up

Instrument boom

Long aerials

You can make your own space probe from simple household items, such as a paper plate, straws and cardboard boxes.

1 First make the probe body by sticking cardboard boxes, tubes and straws together, as shown. **2** Make the dish aerial from the paper plate covered with silver foil. **3** Stick the probe body to the dish aerial. **4** Make the radio pick-up in front of the dish from a triangle of straws and stick it to the dish as shown. **5** Add the long aerials and instrument boom, also made from straws. **6** Finally, you can paint all the straws and cardboard so that it looks like the real thing!

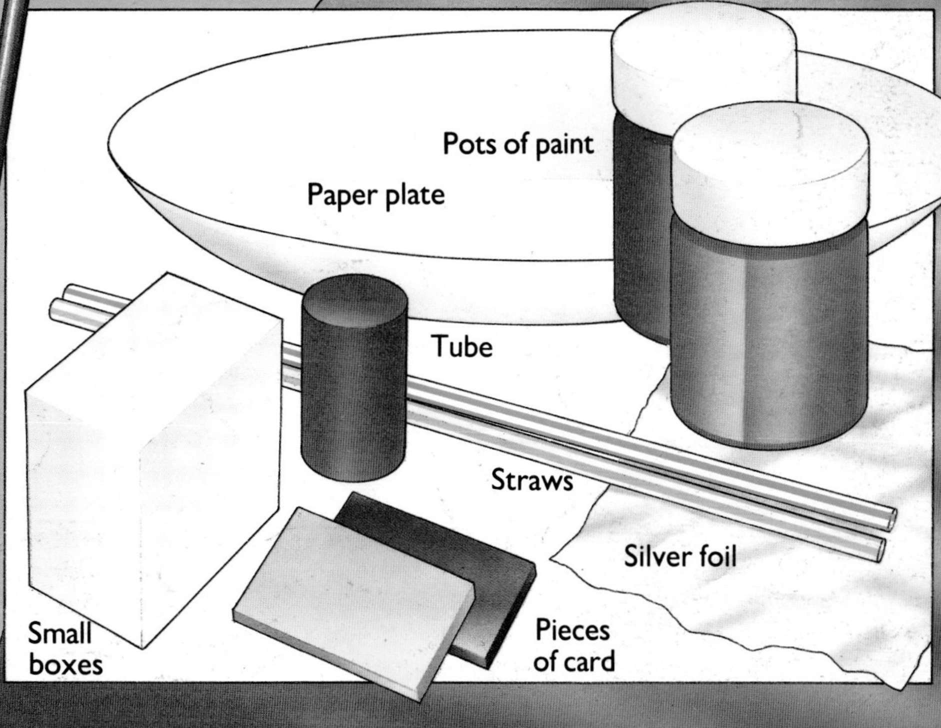

Pots of paint

Paper plate

Tube

Straws

Silver foil

Small boxes

Pieces of card

A Journey Through our Solar System

Ever since modern rockets were developed in the 1950s, people have imagined journeys to distant planets. This true-to-life story is set in the year 2050 when it is expected that space travel will be quite commonplace.

"Crossing Saturn's orbit," the ship's electronic voice purrs from the loudspeaker in the corner of the cabin. Most of the passengers go to the windows, hoping to catch a glimpse of the ringed planet. The passengers are all Science Officers who are returning to Earth after a five-year tour of duty at the Deep Space Observatory. This is a space station permanently in orbit around the planet Neptune.

They are travelling in the ferrycraft, *Solar Explorer 2*. The spacecraft's engines work by heating liquid hydrogen in a nuclear reactor. The engines provide the initial acceleration to move the craft out of Neptune's orbit and to make course corrections, but for most of the journey, the craft 'coasts' unpowered. It uses the pull of gravity of the various planets to help bring it back to Earth.

Hydrogen-powered turbines generate the craft's electricity. Closer to the Sun, solar panels can be used, but in the outer reaches of the Solar System there is not enough light for them to work efficiently.

The cylindrical middle section of the 150 m (500 foot)-long spacecraft spins just fast enough to produce a force similar to Earth's gravity against its outer wall. To the people on board this section, 'up' is towards the centre of the spacecraft. However, the flight deck, where the Pilot, Commander and Engineering Officer work, does not spin. As these members of the crew are consequently weightless, they have to be strapped into their seats while they work.

"Over here," shouts someone. The passengers all rush to the windows. In the far distance, Saturn lies like a glowing golden ball on a black velvet sheet. Its flattened disc of rings is tipped over towards the spacecraft, showing off the rings at their best. The spacecraft's forward video camera slowly rotates to point at the planet. The screen shows that there

are actually hundreds of bright rings packed closely together.

The flight attendant explains that they will not be so lucky with the next planet – Jupiter. By the time they reach Jupiter's orbit, the planet will be hundreds of millions of kilometres away on the other side of the Sun.

"It's going to be a long trip then," says one passenger.

The attendant nods. "Yes, flight time is estimated at 1,735 days – that's four years and nine months." Jupiter is so massive that the extra acceleration from its gravitation field can make all the difference between a short and a long voyage.

The image of Saturn disappears from the viewing screen and a film begins. It is one of several safety and training films shown to every group of

passengers. The passengers return to their seats and the presenter explains the next stage of the flight.

"We will soon begin reducing speed to prepare for the asteroid belt." This is a region of space between the orbits of Mars and Jupiter, where countless millions of rocks orbit the Sun. It is a very dangerous area for any spacecraft. "In three hours we will make a course correction that will pitch us up over the densest region of the belt," the presenter continues. "We will maintain our reduced speed until the positions and trajectories of all large objects in our vicinity are mapped. We will then be able to enter the asteroid field at the safest moment."

During an average journey through the asteroid belt, perhaps two dozen

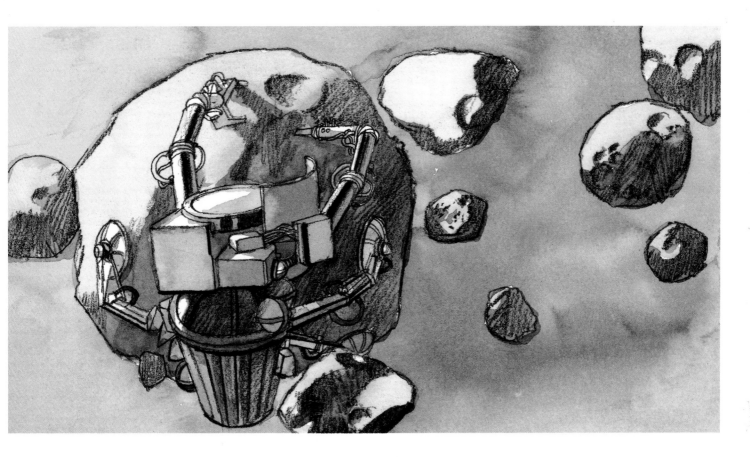

large chunks of rock come within sight of the spacecraft. These and many smaller objects are tracked on radar to ensure that none endanger the spacecraft.

The viewing screen begins to show a film of a journey through the asteroid belt on a previous flight. Large boulders glide across the screen. Some are as big as small planets. A small grey spacecraft is highlighted against the yellow background of one of the larger asteroids.

"That's a miner," says one of the passengers. Asteroids rich in valuable minerals are mined by a fleet of mining craft. These operate from mother-ships lying in safer space outside the asteroid belt. Once safely through the belt, *Solar Explorer 2* sets course for Mars.

On such a long journey, passengers often become very bored. There is nothing to see through the observation windows apart from the occasional close approach to a planet. For most of the journey, there is nothing but darkness and stars outside.

Radio messages take so long to travel from Earth to the craft that two-way conversations are impossible. Most passengers record messages to be transmitted to Earth and busy themselves with reading, games or watching video films while they wait for replies.

To make the journey pass more quickly, passengers can apply for a sleep pattern regulation programme. By wearing a cap fitted with electrodes, the passenger's brain waves can be modified to make him or her sleep longer – up to several days at a time – with no ill effects.

Soon after crossing the orbit of Mars, sleep pattern regulation is brought to an end to give passengers plenty of time to adjust to normal day/night cycles before they reach Earth. At its closest approach to Mars, Earth is only 56 million kilometres (35 million miles) away. The journey is nearing its end.

In common with all interplanetary spacecraft, the *Solar Explorer* will not land on Earth. It was not designed to withstand the high temperatures and forces experienced by a spacecraft entering a planet's atmosphere.

Instead, it will dock with a space station in orbit around Earth. The passengers will then transfer to a shuttle craft for the last stage of the journey to Earth.

Excitement grows among the passengers as the Earth comes into view and two-way radio conversations become possible. The other planets of the Solar System that the *Solar Explorer* has passed by are either violently stormy, hostile worlds or dead chunks of cratered rock. Compared to them, the bright blue sphere of the temperate Earth covered by curling white swirls of cloud looks very welcoming.

TRUE OR FALSE?

Which of these facts are true and which ones are false? If you have read this book carefully, you will know the answers.

1. Our Solar System consists of the Sun, the planets, their moons and all the other objects trapped by the Sun's gravity.

2. The inner planets, the four planets that are closest to the Sun, are all small rocky worlds.

3. Jupiter is such a massive planet that it contains more material than all the other planets added together.

4. The visible surface of the Sun is called the photosphere.

6. The Earth's Moon always shows the same face to the Earth because the Moon does not spin round.

7. Saturn's famous rings are solid discs of frozen hydrogen and water-ice mixed with particles of dust blown by winds.

5. The Sun is a huge ball of gases. It contains a wide variety of different gases, but it consists mostly of carbon dioxide and oxygen.

8. The ocean tides are caused by the solar wind blowing water against the shore.

9. Most of the asteroids in our Solar System lie between the orbits of Mars and Jupiter.

GLOSSARY

● **Atmosphere** is a layer of gas that surrounds some stars, planets and moons. The Earth's atmosphere is roughly four-fifths nitrogen and one-fifth oxygen, with tiny amounts of a few other gases. Other planets have different atmospheres.

● **Atoms** are the smallest parts of a material that can take part in chemical reactions.

● **Comets** are small balls of dusty ice that orbit the Sun. As they approach the Sun and are heated by it, gases evaporate from them and form a long tail.

● **Diameter** is the width of a circle or sphere (ball). Planets are not perfect spheres – their diameter is measured across the equator.

● **Earthquakes** are a violent shaking of the Earth's surface, caused by brittle rocks in the Earth's crust breaking up as plates in the crust move against each another.

● **Energy** enables things and living creatures to do work. There are many different forms of energy including heat, light, sound, electrical and chemical energy.

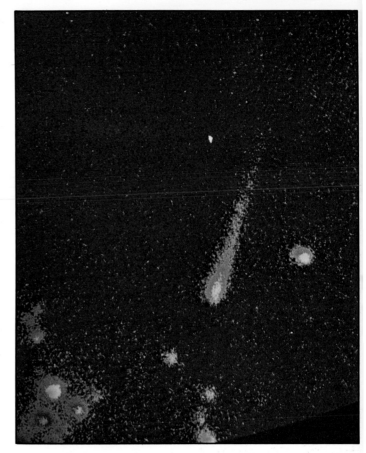

▲ Comet Kohoutek (in the centre) photographed on Christmas Day in 1973 from Skylab, high above the Earth's atmosphere.

● **Equator** is an imaginary line around a planet, midway between its north and south poles.

● **Gravity** is a force that attracts objects to each other. It pulls us down towards the Earth's surface. The more massive the object, the greater is its force of gravity.

● **Magnetic field** is a region of space where the effect of a magnet exists.

● **Milky Way** is the star system, or galaxy, our Solar System belongs to.

▲ The planet Saturn with its rings and moons. This scene was compiled from Voyager 1 spacecraft photos.

● **Moons** are the natural objects that orbit a planet.

● **Radar** is a system used to detect and locate objects that are either too far away to be seen, or are hidden.

● **Volcanoes** are holes in a planet's crust where molten rock may spew out.

SYSTEM FACTS

● Our Solar System condensed from a swirling cloud of dust and gas in one of the arms of a spiral galaxy called the **Milky Way** about 15 thousand million years ago.

● Neptune's largest moon, Triton, is falling towards Neptune. In 10 to 100 million years, Triton will collide with the planet.

● The planet with the strongest gravity is, not surprisingly, also the biggest – Jupiter. The force of gravity at Jupiter's surface is 2.64 times the Earth's. Someone weighing 50 kg (110 pounds) on Earth would weigh over 130 kg (290 pounds) on Jupiter.

● The closest star to the Sun is Proxima Centauri, a small cool type of star called a 'red dwarf'. It would take 4.3 years to reach it travelling at the speed of light.

● The closer a planet is to the Sun, the shorter is its year. Mercury's year is 88 Earth-days long. Pluto's is 248 Earth-years long. Earth, which lies between the two, has 365.25 days in a year.

● The Voyager spacecraft discovered that in addition to Saturn, whose rings had already been seen from Earth, Jupiter, Uranus and Neptune also are encircled by rings.

INDEX